How to Design Your
TRADING

7 THINGS YOU MUST HAVE IN YOUR TRADING PLAN.

AYOWOLE AMPITAN

DEDICATION

This book is dedicated to every trader who want to boost their discipline, confidence and profitability in the financial market.

ACKNOWLEDGEMENTS

This is a concerted efforts of many great minds and a compilation of their insights. Thank you to my friend and brother Anthony Amos, Pst Tobi Ampitan. Thank you to Aramide Opayemi who proofread and edit the book. Thank you to Penuel Forex Family especially to Joseph Monyei, eto solomon, and Skyhigh, your insights were helpful. Thank you to all my proteges. Thank God for wisdom and strength.

Date of Publication: November, 2022

Published by Ayowole Ampitan

Edited by: Aramide Opayemi

Publishers; ayodejiampitan@gmail.com; +2348133558222.

NB: Most time no matter how you sieve out stones and sand from Rice or beans, one or two stones will still be found in it. Same goes to proofread and editing a book, after working on it you might still find where we ought to put comma and we didn't put or some typographical error. Please do bear with us but I assure you that you will get massive value and clarity in this book.

FOREWORD

Trading can be very complicated; it is not easy but can be simplified when you keep it simple.

In this Book "**HOW TO DESIGN YOUR TRADING PLAN**" Ayowole Ampitan has broken down everything a trader need, to be highly profitable and consistent in the long run.

Please follow it religiously because your trading success largely depend on this.

Truth be told, only traders that have a strict trading plan would last in the business.

Remember, "If you failed to plan, you have planned to fail"

Cheers

Tobi Ampitan

Inventor, Traffic FX

Expert News trader

REVIEWS AND COMMENTS ABOUT THE BOOK

This is a laudable initiative and very necessary for all retail traders.

Ejimi olufukeji Adegbeye

Africa's no. 1 profitable investor.

Wowww❤️🖤❤️🖤 this is an awesome piece.

Very well curated and written.

The ideas and instructions are perfectly passed to the audience and the flow is great.

You did a very good job.

This is a book I will highly recommend to every trader out there.

You asked me to review and give feedback, but honestly after reading this I became a benefactor.

I love that you didn't just outline what traders need to do but you also gave simple examples that can help even the newest trader comprehend and apply.

This is very commendable as not everyone can write such details with such simplicity.

I love everything about the book.

I love that the message was brief yet concise.

I love how reading every page comes with ease.

I can't wait to get a hard copy for myself.

Binjo Haye

FX Trader

I've read the book and honestly it is a masterpiece. I even find it more than just about a trading plan because it encompasses a lot of ideas that could generally impact how a person analyse the charts in a positive way.

To me it's more than just a trading plan guide, it is a guide to making better analysis generally which covers from the psychological aspect down to the charts and even chart correlations.

Kimie Alexander

FX Trader

INTRODUCTION

WARNING

The ideas in this book can be hazardous to mediocrity, average and unprofitability in your trading.

I won't bore you with long stories. As your co-trader in this industry, I believe you don't need some sort of cock and bull stories.

The desire of every trader is profitability in the long run.

Trading is a business, so you have to treat it as such if you want to succeed. Every business person wants to be profitable.

However, some tidbits need to be put in place to ensure profitability.

I know you must have heard of the phrase "If you fail to plan, you plan to fail".

If you are serious about being successful in any business in which trading is not an exception, you should follow those words blindly as if they were inscribed on stone.

If you don't follow a well-written trading plan, you are doomed to fail every single time you try to trade any market.

Traders who win consistently treat trading as a business. While it's not a guarantee that you will make money, having a plan is crucial if you want to become consistently successful and survive in the trading game.

The book in your hands is a masterpiece that will aid your profitability and consistency. Read it meditatively and take action on it immediately, remember, reading without applying is as good as not picking up the book.

Let's journey together. It promises to be a fruitful one.

Cheers!

WHAT TRADING PLAN IS ABOUT

A trading plan defines what is supposed to be done, why, when, and how. It covers your trader personality, personal expectations, risk management rules, and trading system(s).

A trading plan is a comprehensive decision-making tool for your trading activity. It is a set of rules guiding a trader's trading activity.

When religiously followed, a trading plan will help limit trading mistakes and minimize your losses. It helps you decide what, when, and how much to trade.

A trading plan should be your own, personal plan – you could use someone else's plan as an outline but remember that we all have different attitudes toward things. So, that person's attitude towards risk and available capital could be vastly different from yours.

A trading plan is to ensure utmost discipline and profitability.

A trading plan removes any bad decision-making in the heat of the moment.

Your emotions can consume you when money is on the line, causing you to make irrational decisions. You don't want that to happen, right?

The best way to prevent it from happening is to minimize it, by having a plan for every potential market action.

With the right trading plan, every action is spelled out, so that you don't have to make any rash decisions in the heat of the moment.

A trading plan specifies a trader's entry, exit, and money management criteria for every trade

If you make your trade plan in advance, your overall approach is less likely to be influenced by the market occurrences that can, and probably will affect your thinking after the trade is placed.

Not only that, but you are also less likely to let your emotions gain control of your trade execution.

A plan should be crafted out on paper before you start trading, but it should always be subject to reevaluation.

A trading plan is subject to change as the trader's skill level and understanding of the market improves.

The key is to stick to the plan. Taking trades outside the trading plans is considered a poor strategy and indiscipline, even if it turns out a win.

In simple words, stick to your trading plan.

The Difference between a Trading Plan and a Trading System

Before we proceed, let's quickly distinguish between a trading plan and a trading system.

1. A trading system describes how you will enter and exit trades.

2. A trading system is PART of your trading plan but is just one of several important parts, i.e., analysis, executions, risk management, etc.

A trading plan is different from a trading strategy, which defines precisely how you should enter and exit trades.

An example of a simple trading strategy would be 'buy bitcoin when it reaches $5000 and sell when it reaches $6000'.

WHY DO YOU NEED A TRADING PLAN?

You need a trading plan because it can help you make logical trading decisions and define the parameters of your ideal trade.

A good trading plan will help you to avoid making emotional decisions in the heat of the moment. The benefits of a trading plan include:

- **Made trading easy**: It is easier to do a thing when you know how it should be and must be done.

  Trading plan lays out all the criteria that must be met before any trading decision is made.

  It will always point you in the right direction no matter the distractions present.

  All the planning has been done upfront, so you can trade according to your pre-set parameters

- **Help make more objective decisions**: Trading is about decisions. Good decisions will make you money, while bad decisions will cost you money.

  As a trader, you will know when you should take a profit and cut losses, which means you can take emotions out of your decision-making process.

- **Better trading discipline**: Trading is a marathon, not a sprint. It is important to have and build a solid trading plan and follow it with religious discipline throughout your entire trading activity.

  By sticking to your plan with discipline, you could discover why certain trades work and others don't.

- **Room for improvement**: One of the core components of a trading plan is a trading journal, which is essentially a diary or record of your trading activity.

  Journaling your trading activity will help you to assess the performance of your trading strategies as well as other factors of your trading plan, such as risk management and trading psychology.

  This will highlight the areas where improvements can be made to help you become a better trader.

  Defining your record-keeping procedure enables you to learn from past trading mistakes and improve your judgment.

HOW TO DEVELOP YOUR TRADING PLAN

We have established in the previous chapters what a trading plan is all about and the benefits of developing a personal and solid trading plan.

We have different market perspectives, experiences, and thought processes, so it's not advisable to blindly copy another person's trading plan.

It is important to have your personalized trading plan and update it as you learn from the market

Developing a trading plan and sticking to it are the two main ingredients of discipline in trading.

There are components that make a good trading plan.

Every component must constitute your trading plan if your desired destination as a trader is profitability.

In this chapter, I will be sharing concisely 7 things you must have in your trading plan.

I will break them down into nuggets so you can easily read and digest them.

I might not arrange them in order of priority because each of them is equally important. None is greater than the other.

CHAPTER ONE

MARKET AND ASSET CLASSES

We all know that a market is where **buying** and **selling** happens, there are also **products** being traded in a market;

In a financial market, there are "**Products**" being traded, some of which are;

1. CURRENCIES

2. COMMODITIES

3. CRYPTO-CURRENCIES

4. STOCKS

5. DERIVATIVES etc.

6. INDICES

The details of your trading plan will be affected by the market you want to trade. For instance, a forex trading plan will be different from a stock trading plan.

To begin with, evaluate your expertise when it comes to asset classes and markets, and learn as much as you can about the one (market) you want to trade. Then, observe when the market opens and closes, the volatility of the market, and how much you stand to lose or gain per point of movement in the price. If you're not certain about all these, you might want to choose a different market that you understand.

You have to decide on the market you want to trade in and the asset classes.

1. CURRENCIES:

The world has more than 100 CURRENCIES and a handful of them have been paired in the forex market for trading.

¶Examples of currency pairs are:

•EUR/USD

•GBP/JPY

•AUD/CAD

2. COMMODITIES:

Commodities are also traded in the forex market, examples are

- Gold
- Silver
- Platinum
- Oil

- Gas. Etc.

3. CRYTPOCURRENCIES: digital currencies are also traded in the FX MARKET, e.g., BTC (bitcoin), ETH (Ethereum), XRP (ripple), etc.

4. STOCKS:

Stocks are shares of companies being represented in terms of price, they show the overall performance of a company over time, and these relative performances can be traded.

You can find them in the forex market being traded against the dollar.

Examples of the stock market are; Facebook, Amazon, Google, Netflix, etc.

5. DERIVATIVES: These are new instruments introduced into the markets, based purely on supply and demand, they aren't attached to any company/country or organization,

And they can be traded every day on MT5.

¶ Examples are Volatility indices, Crash/boom index, STEP INDEX, etc.

6. INDICES:

Indices are the opposite of stocks.

They are like a collection of similar companies being represented as one in terms of overall performance.

For example, the top 100 tech companies in America are represented as NAS100 (NASDAQ100).

So, their overall performances will be represented in a single chart.

Other examples are:

*FTSE

*DAX100

*US30

*S&P500

I often advise my students to focus on JUST ONE MARKET and 2-3 assets.

For example; I focus on the currencies market and the assets I focus on are; XAUUSD, EUR, and USD.

I believe as you are reading you are already deciding the market and assets you want to focus on perhaps based on your experience or the one that appeals to your personality or trading style.

Do your homework well and decide on the market and asset you want to trade.

CHAPTER TWO

RISK MANAGEMENT

Trading knowledge including technical analysis, good strategies, and chart reading is all necessary but alone is not enough to make you a successful trader.

Risk management is the foundation of a successful trading system.

Risk management in trading could be a deciding factor in whether you're a consistently profitable trader or, a losing trader.

Remember, you can have the best trading strategy in the world but without being able to properly manage risk, you may not rise beyond your level of understanding.

I won't be teaching in-depth on risk management but I will share what you must include in a risk management plan as part of a trading plan.

What you must include in the Risk management plan

- **The level of risk-to-reward ratio you are working on in each trade.**

  Risk is defined as the amount a trader is willing to lose on a trade if it hits his or her stop. Calculate risk on trade (size of a stop) by measuring the distance between entry and stop-loss.

  The reward is simply defined as the price distance between our entry and our profit point. The trading risk-reward ratio simply determines the potential loss (risk) versus the potential profit (reward) on any given trade.

To calculate your desired risk-reward ratio, compare the amount of money you want to risk on each trade to the potential gain. If your maximum potential loss is $200 and the maximum potential gain is $600, the risk-reward ratio is 1:3.

For me, it is not a good trade or setup if it doesn't give 1:2 or 1:3. 3 to 1, that is, exit once a profit of three times the risk has been reached, for instance, if you risk $4, exit once the profit is $12.

- **The maximum percentage of your account that you are willing to risk on any trade.**

The recommended risk per trade is 1% or less of your account size or capital. Risk a maximum of 1% of your account per trade or risk 0.5% and take twice the trades with half the risk.

- **The maximum position size per trade.**

I have seen many traders open 10 positions on a setup or pairs. I won't talk down on them but make sure that you spread the 1% risk of your equity on the number of positions you open; which means you won't be risking 1% on each of them.

Setting the maximum number of trades open at any one time is directly related to your monthly drawdown. You must have a way to limit the number of trades that can be triggered at any given moment, or else you might end up with several losses that will exceed your maximum drawdown.

Consider this scenario, you have established a 5% maximum drawdown, you risk 1% on each trade and you are allowed to have 5 trades open at the same time. If you trade more than 5 trades at 1%, risks are open and your drawdown might end up being 6% or more. If you are risking 0.5% on each trade, you are allowed to have 10 trades open at the same time.

Decide the maximum position size per trade setup.

- **Maximum daily, weekly and monthly drawdown**

Set Maximum Monthly Drawdown!

Risk management will make money for you in the long run, but there is always another side to things. What would happen if you didn't use strict risk management rules?

Consider this example: Let's say you have $10,000 and you lose $5,000. What percentage of your account have you lost? The answer is 50%. Simple enough. That's what we call drawdown.

A drawdown is the reduction of one's capital after a series of losing trades during a specific period. This is normally calculated by getting the difference between relative peaks in capital minus a relative trough. We normally note this down as a percentage of their trading account.

You can set the overall drawdown (loss) as 10% while the daily or weekly drawdown of your account is 5%.

If the overall drawdown is reached, stop trading for that month and it's advisable to stop trading when the daily or weekly drawdown is reached.

It doesn't make you a bad trader, market conditions might just not be favorable.

My mentor, **OLUWATOBI AMPITAN,** suggests a maximum drawdown of 30-50% of your equity. According to him, "having a maximum account drawdown will help your discipline and risk management as a trader".

You must trade like a professional, a professional trader will establish a maximum monthly drawdown and respect it. His career and success depend on it.

- **Your monthly target.**

  Many aspiring traders have an unrealistic target.

  They start with a $5,000 account and expect to make $5,000 in their first month of trading. No wonder many traders fail.

  Set a realistic monthly target and stop trading when you reach your target.

CHAPTER THREE

METHOD OF TRADING.

One of the most important components of your trading plan is the **strategy, concept, and system** used to approach the market or trade in the market.

There is no new thing in the market but your **perspectives**. The way you view the market.

Every trader has what they look out for on the chart before they place a trade. You must develop your skills as a trader and your edge.

Your trading strategy must be systematic.

There are three main systematic process of trading.

    a) Directional bias.

    b) Area of interest

    c) Entry trigger.

1) **Directional bias:** What do you use to gauge the direction of the market? Examples are; INDEX, STRUCTURE, and EMA

2) **Area of interest:** This defines where you want to get involved in the market.

Do you want to trade order block? Stick to it!

Do you want to trade support and resistance? Stick to it!

Do you want to trade supply and demand? Stick to it!

Do you want to trade the Fibonacci level? Stick to it!

Whatever method you have chosen just stick to it and wait for the price to come to your point of interest. If the price doesn't come do not force it. Obey your plan, stick to your plan, and follow your plan. Do not try to catch the move!

That price doesn't respect your POI doesn't mean it's a bad trade or a bad analysis. Out of every 10setups, at least 6-7 setups can be assured to be a win.

3) **Entry Trigger**: This is simply the mode of entry. There are two ways to trigger a trade.

(a) Candlestick formation (direct Entry): It is a confirmatory entry. i.e., engulfing pattern, pin bar, hammer, and others.

(b) Limit orders: This is another mode of placing a trade at your POI (in the expectation that the price will get there) activate it and go in your anticipated direction. Examples are; Buy stop, sell stop, buy limit and Sell limit.

Monthly and Weekly timeframe shows you the overall direction and trend of the pair. Always follow the trend.

Know your **area of interest** then wait for **entry confirmation** before you pull the trigger.

A trading strategy mustn't be complex to make you money. It can be as simple as ABC and still be profitable.

Trading the financial market is delicate just as flying an aircraft is to every pilot, but having and sticking to the checklist will make the difference and guarantee a safe flight.

To be a profitable trader, you must be strategic.

Are you ready to trade strategically?

Have you back-test the strategy?

Are you confident that it works?

Can you follow your own trading decisions without any form of hesitation?

Always bear in mind that professionals trade based on probabilities and an edge. They don't gamble.

CHAPTER FOUR

TIME COMMITMENT

Set a maximum number of hours to trade a day

The time variable is key to trading, it can lead to over-analysis.

To prevent that from happening, you must set a maximum number of times you'll spend in front of the charts. If it's 1 hour or 2 hours a day, do it and be consistent with it. Set that limit and stop analyzing the markets once that deadline has been achieved.

Deliberately work out how much time you can commit to your trading activities.

Set aside enough time to monitor your trades but consider what time of day will work best for you.

Some traders prefer to keep an eye on their trades all day, while others set aside sometime in the morning, during the day, and in the evening.

It is advisable that you manage your risk with stops, but this is especially true if you plan to keep positions open when you will not be monitoring them.

Select your Trading Sequence and Entry Timeframe

You know there are different timeframes you can trade, you can hold a trade for hours, days, even weeks and months. First of all, you should decide which type of trader you are, select your entry timeframe and that will be a law!.

You have a few choices: longer-term, swing, and intraday/scalping.

Let me give you few useful tips on the timeframe you should consider.

- Daily timeframe shows the trend of the month.
- 4-hour timeframe shows the trend of the week.
- 1-hour timeframe shows the trend of the daily timeframe for intraday trading.

Market Condition

One of the most important things you must factor into your trading plan is the market condition, in terms of days that there's low or high volatility in the market.

Some traders have strict plans not to trade on Monday because of slow market conditions and Friday cause of volatile conditions.

While some traders during high-impact news week, won't even take a glance at the chart.

One major problem is that most traders want to focus on every market condition.

It's more like focusing on different timeframes without strict rules surrounding the timeframe that fits your trading approach.

Swing

Scalp

Intraday.

You want to trade everything

It is best to choose your trading style and stick to it then know the timeframe that suits your trading style.

For monthly swing, you do your analysis monthly then the daily timeframe is your entry.

For weekly swing, you do your analysis on a weekly timeframe then your entry timeframe is H4.

If you do your analysis on a daily timeframe, your entry timeframe is 1hr for intraday trading.

Ensure to choose a framework that best fits your trading style.
We'll highlight the trading style on the next page.

CHAPTER FIVE

TRADING STYLE

Decide what type of trader you are. Your trading style should be based on your personality, your attitude toward risk, as well as the amount of time you're willing to commit to trading. There are four main trading styles:

- **Position trading**: holding positions for weeks, months, or years with the expectation that they will become profitable in the long term

- **Swing trading**: holding positions over several days or weeks, to take advantage of medium-term market moves

- **Day trading**: opening and closing a small number of trades on the same day and not holding any positions overnight, eliminating some costs and risks

- **Scalping**: placing several trades per day, for a few seconds or minutes, in an attempt to make small profits that add up to a large amount.

SCALPING	DAY TRADING	SWING TRADING
5mins-30mins	1hr-4hr	6hrs-1D

Most time who introduced you to trading determines your style of trading or perhaps by virtue of experience you have been able to spot the style that suits your personality.

I choose certain concept or trading approach because it suits my personality.

So, my style of trading instills in me Patience, Contentment and attention to details.

If I am trading a SUPPLY & DEMAND zone, I won't take or trade all supply or demand zones I see on the chart.

I will have to check for which is strong and offer a high probability.

Once I spot it, I put pending order and wait for price to come to my kill zone.

I just showed you a glimpse of how I trade.

CHAPTER SIX

Daily routine and trade preparation

Executing a daily routine is key to your trading success.

You are already executing a bunch of habits and routines every single day of your life.

You wake up at 7 a.m. have breakfast, read your favorite newspaper, drive to work, have lunch at 1 pm, etc.

Your trading space (area) should not suffer any distractions.

Remember, this is a business and distractions can be costly. You must create new habits and a daily routine for your trading.

Without a daily trading routine, you may find it difficult to find a foot in trading the financial market.

Top athletes perform well because they have rituals and routines for every single thing they do in life.

I think we can all agree that habits are what determine our success or failure in any endeavor or challenge in our lives.

Trading is not an exception. How do we develop the type of habits that will lead us to become profitable traders? The answer is straightforward: Routine.

Proper trading habits do not just magically appear out of the blue.

These habits can sometimes take years to form. Not everything is lost, you have the power to come up with a plan and put it into motion, a plan that will bring forth the proper trading habits.

The development of positive habits, the ones that lead to success in any field, is something you can make a conscious effort to achieve simply by implementing consistent daily routines.

When you think about your daily trading routine, what do you think about it?

Do you even have one?

Are you aware that professionals, not only professional traders but lawyers, and doctors, have strict routines whether they realize it or not?

They follow these plans and routines like clockwork, everything from diet, exercise, sleep, and meditation. One thing that any successful professional has in common is that they have gone from daily routines to ingraining those habits that virtually guarantee consistent and ongoing success in their field.

I am not talking about just having a trading plan either. I'm talking about what you do from the time you wake up to the time you sleep, this is all part of your daily trading routine.

Professional traders have developed a daily routine that maximizes their ability to trade successfully.

This routine can take you about 1-2 hours every day, some days it could be less, about 30 to 60 minutes maximum. It will depend on how many assets class (EUR/USD) and which entry timeframe you are trading, as well as how experienced you are.

Template for a daily routine

You have to treat trading as a business. The way you write the to-do lists that made you disciplined, effective, and productive in other aspects of your life is the same way you should treat your trading daily routine.

For example;

• *I wake up at 6:00-6:30 am.*

• *My analysis and trading come at 7:00 am. I do not go back to check live charts until the next trading day. I do not modify any of my existing orders. Once I'm done for the day, my office is closed.*

• *I focus only on assets that are trending.*

• I am only allowed to trade for 1 hour a day.

• Update the trading community and reply to chats from 7:00 am to 8:30 am.

• Switch to mobile mode. Keep on replying to urgent posts from my mobile after 8:30 am.

• Since I am only trading currency and synthetics, I will be available when the US market opens, IF and only if, I need to plan or manage a trade.

• Enjoy the rest of the day doing the things I love to do.

• Allocate some time for back-testing the rules.

• I'm allowed to do all -ing (singing, playing, and reading) activities except trading.

• I do not have any applications on my mobile to keep track of my trades, I simply allow my trade to run.

Your routine might be different from the one above. However, it seeks to give an insight into how yours is expected to look.

CHAPTER SEVEN

JOURNAL YOUR TRADES

For a trading plan to work, it needs to be backed up by a trading journal. You should use your trading diary to document your trades as this can help you find out what's working and what isn't.

You don't only have to include the technical details, such as the entry and exit points of the trade, but also the rationale behind your trading decisions and emotions. If you deviate from your plan, write down why you did it and what the outcome was. The more detail in your journal, the better.

Keep a detailed journal of all your trading activities. This is before you enter a trade, during the trade, and even after the trade is closed.

Record your reasons to enter and exit any trade, as well as the targets and underlying emotions or psychological feelings during every stage of your trading activity.

If you want to succeed in your trading business, be an excellent accountant – record everything!

TRADING JOURNAL TEMPLATE

S/N	DATE	MARKET SESSION	ASSET	LOT SIZE	HTF SETUP
1					
2					
3					
4					

LTF CONFIRMATION	SL (PIPS	TP(PIPS)	RR RATIO	OUTCOME	COMMENTS

Always keep the BEFORE and AFTER of your trades. Open a special folder where you save them.

Document flashcards of your trades. It will boost your confidence and help you track your progress.

FINAL WORDS

I am super excited that I wrote this book for you. I believe when the components are well-knitted, they will form a masterpiece that increases your discipline and profitability.

I desire that you become a better and more profitable trader. You are the real MVP.

 I am rooting for you!

Author Contact

AMPITAN AYOWOLE is a Forex trader and financial market analyst.

His writings and speaking prowess are Juggernaut and topnotch.

He is a Business freak Nigerian that has a vast knowledge and experience in Sales and Marketing, Branding, Copywriting and Business growth.

He is a simple, humble, meek, and hospitable Man.

He has the passion and drive to impact lives positively and see everyone that comes around him transformed.

AYOWOLE AMPITAN welcomes the opportunity to speak at churches, conferences, and various business settings. For more information, to schedule **AYOWOLE AMPITAN** to speak, or for ONE-ON-ONE coaching and mentorship services,

please contact: **AYOWOLE AMPITAN**

08133558222, ayodejiampitan@gmail.com